All
Occasions

ALL
OCCASIONS

Walt McDonald

University of Notre Dame Press
Notre Dame, Indiana

Copyright 2000 by
University of Notre Dame Press
Notre Dame, Indiana 46556
All Rights Reserved
http://www.undpress.nd.edu

Manufactured in the United States of America

Library of Congress Cataloging-in-Publication Data
McDonald, Walter.
All occasions / Walt McDonald.
p.   cm.
ISBN 0-268-02005-1 (cloth : alk. paper)
ISBN 0-268-02006-X (pbk. : alk. paper)
I. Title.
PS3563.A2914. A78   2000
811'.54—dc21   00-056800

∞ *This book is printed on acid-free paper.*

All occasions invite his mercies, and all times are his seasons.

— John Donne, *LXXX Sermons*, 3,
preached on Christmas Day, 1624

Contents

2. When Rockets Fell like Stars

3. Wishing for Friends from Childhood

4. Search and Rescue

5. East of Eden

Acknowledgments

I'm deeply grateful to editors of the following publications in which earlier versions of these poems first appeared, some with different titles:

Alaska Quarterly Review:
    "I Still Can't Say the Word"
America:
    "The Last Pullman to Houston"
American Literary Review:
    "As Time Goes By"
    "Barter"
Bottomfish:
    "When Baseball Was a Game"
Buffalo Spree:
    "All Dogs Are Pirates"
The Cape Rock:
    "Fire and Ice"
Chelsea:
    "At Dawn with the Blinds Raised"
    "Diamonds in the Carnegie Museum"

The Christian Century:
"Before the Glaciers Melt"
"Faith Is a Radical Master"
Clackamas Literary Review:
"A Thousand Miles of Stars"
College English:
"After the Children Leave"
Confrontation:
"Marching through Georgia"
Connecticut Review:
"Wishing for Friends from Childhood"
Connecticut River Review:
"Swaggering to the Flight Line"
Dalhousie Review (Canada):
"Grandfathers"
The Distillery:
"Gigging for Frogs before the War"
Farmer's Market [now *Black Dirt*]:
"Beside the Dark-Sheened Water"
First Things:
"Instant Replay"
"Leaving Sixty"
"When Rockets Fell like Stars"
The Formalist:
"Uncle Croom's Attic"
Fox Cry Review:
"Cousin Eddie and the Jungle Trails"
Illinois Review:
"Boys and Their Fathers' Shotguns"
Image:
"Watching Parades in the Game Room"
JAMA: The Journal of the American Medical Association:
"Facing It"
"For Friends Missing in Action"
"Grandfather and the Boys He Knew in School"
"The Risk of Having Children"
"The Summer Her Family Moved to Houston"
"Watching Dawn on Padre Island"

Literature & Belief:
"My Father and the Sad Soap Operas"
"Search and Rescue in the Mountains"

Louisiana Literature:
"John Parker and the Captured Mount"

Mid-American Review:
"One Steep Switchback at a Time"

The Missouri Review:
"After the Random Tornado"
"But It Was Water"
"That Silence When a Mountain Lion Attacks"
"The Songs of Country Girls"

The National Forum:
"One Morning between Wars"

The New Criterion:
"Growing Up by the Brazos"

New Millennium Writings:
"Abandoned Shack in Bankhead National Forest"

New Texas 95:
"To the Tribe"

North Dakota Quarterly:
"The Second Time Around"

Outerbridge:
"Chocolate"

Prairie Schooner:
"Old Pilots in the Crowd at Kitty Hawk"

The Sewanee Review:
"Batting Practice at Sixty"
"Killing Nothing but Time"

Shenandoah:
"Boiling Shells at Kitty Hawk"

South Carolina Review:
"Raising a Glass for Grandsons"

South Dakota Review:
"800 Acres on the Plains"

Southern Poetry Review:
"In the Alchemist's Household"

Staple (U.K.):
"Backpacking with My Bride in the Rockies"
Tar River Poetry:
"Wings Tumbling like a Torch"
Weber Studies:
"In the Shallow Molasses"
Windhover:
"The Midas Touch in Texas"
Writer's Forum:
"Hardscrabble, Tooth and Claw"
Zone 3:
"Bogeyman, 1969"

"Old Pilots in the Crowd at Kitty Hawk" is reprinted from *Prairie Schooner* by permission of University of Nebraska Press. Copyright 1999 by University of Nebraska Press.

"Batting Practice at Sixty" and "Killing Nothing but Time" were first published in *The Sewanee Review*, vol. 107, no. 4, Fall 1999. Copyright 1999 by Walter McDonald.

I also thank Wesleyan University Press for permission to quote from James Dickey's "Hunting Civil War Relics at Nimblewill Creek," *The Whole Motion: Collected Poems, 1945–1992* (Middletown, Conn.: Wesleyan University Press, 1992).

ONE

The Midas Touch

I find that I have painted my life—things happening in my life—without knowing. . . . I had to create an equivalent for what I felt about what I was looking at—not copy it.

—Georgia O'Keeffe

One Morning between Wars

The girl in the purple robe
tangled like a bath towel
lolls on the couch and laughs,
some pre-school song or clown trick
bouncing in her mind. Will she

years from now recall this Sunday morning
on the coast, up before Mommy
and her brothers, the lazy, purring world
all to herself? Will she remember
this hour of lounging, twisting

turning, and humming, her daddy
bringing breakfast on a tray,
the brittle bacon, the tiny tub of syrup,
hot strips of sweet French toast?
Will she miss the months he wasn't home,

the TV chant of Desert Storm
that grown-ups found exciting? He's back,
and now she lolls and rolls the bacon
on her lips, and nibbles, dips the toast
and dribbles sticky syrup on her tongue.

Her own real daddy brings
more bacon strips. He says she makes him
happy when she eats so well. Twisting
bacon like a rotor blade, she sings
about her daddy days ago, descending

from the sky like Santa Claus,
leaves blowing everywhere,
the whole crowd waving at her daddy's
helicopter, a real, brave daddy
finally back. She sniffs the bacon,

lips it, sucks it like a lollypop
and hums, God up in heaven,
her daddy close enough to hear her
when she calls, another strip
of French toast in her bowl.

The Second Time Around

If by some tide I had found you strolling,
holding white sandals by the thongs,
what could I have done, assuming someone
husbandly held your other hand like a pearl?

When you said no and flew away, I let you go,
what else? For months, I bored holes
in thunderclouds, flung a jet boldly
over fields and forests, pulled hard

and corkscrewed up at the sun, the wild blue,
not even hoping. Women from Georgia to Hawaii
danced softly in my arms, fondling my silver wings.
Not one of them was you. And then that noon

of now-done longing when I turned and saw you
there on the stairs, staring at me across the hall
before the opera started, startled to find you again,
alone, without a ring, and coming down the stairs.

One Steep Switchback at a Time

Bundled in mohair, we trudge white powder
under pines. Elk watch us, and coyotes
lope boldly through the snow. Cattle caught in the open
freeze without the scruffy coats elk grow.
On that dude ranch, geldings wear quilts

stitched by a Parisian seamstress. Next month, they'll pack
tourists up mountains, families that drive all night
to escape from plains so flat they're blind.
Good horses do what we all do when we get there,
wherever we're going, one steep switchback at a time.

But now, they crush the frozen ruts
of the corral. Split fences hold stiff blizzards
back, pickets bent like bows. Hawks cling
to blue spruce bucking in gusts. Old geldings browse
with icy tails, free at last of flies.

They shake their heads and blink in steamy breaths
and flakes and thrust their bone skulls into hay.
Nowhere to go, like us, they stand all night
and stare, ignoring cold as if they hope
they'll blow those steamy breaths forever.

Backpacking with My Bride in the Rockies

A flick uphill, robin or chipmunk, or bigger.
Outside the tent, the coffee's hot, my wife inside,
asleep. I reach for black binoculars and wait.

Nothing for seconds, then the frantic signals start,
a ground squirrel soprano hitting the high note.
Suddenly, the green slope's littered with lookouts,

rodents stretching tall as eight inches can see
past boulders and a thousand pines. A fox
or coyote is up there prowling, not black bear

or puma, too haughty or cunning for us
with nothing left but hard tack and water,
beef jerky sealed in air-tight plastic and hung

a hundred yards downhill. My wife of five nights
lifts the tent flap and squints, still in her robe.
I have no doubt it's there, coyote or red fox,

wily and starved. I pour a cup that steams
at 10,000' and hand it to my wife.
I marvel at her lips, the tilt of her throat

when she swallows, the taste and curve of her
in a perfect world. Squirrel babies play
and tumble on their holes. The main guard

shrieks her thin, ear-piercing note, tucking her gut
and thrusting a tufted head like a coach
or quarterback. It's a game they play every day,

real bogeymen with fangs that stalk
and test the wind, and even though they pass by now,
detected and warned off, tomorrow they'll be back.

In the Alchemist's Household

Burning coal for gold, my wife
waves our big-eyed children
back from the kiln. Moths
fluttering from joy to joy,

they bob and weave as if she's
a goalie; her studio, a soccer field.
I've seen her spin exquisite vases
from clay, jars of the same sienna sand

we live on. In months, she turned
mere kisses into screams
and tiny fists, squinty infants
who turned her breast milk

into teeth and giggles, into fists
that lifted puppies up and snuggled.
She makes sand paintings
I want to frame and save,

grains of a prairie rainbow
she sweeps at sundown and scatters.
She turns long nights to dawn
by bedsides of the dying,

moans and groaning that hush
when she's beside them in a chair,
stroking their twitching thumbs,
holding their IV hands.

800 Acres on the Plains

Room at the trough, another black calf
missing, fat Angus shoving like hogs for water
in August. Ninety, a hundred, a hundred four.
Somewhere the buzzards pray, maybe bowing bald heads
and feasting, calling hungry cousins to supper.
Nothing to do but saddle a gelding and backtrack range

where the hot herd waddled. I pack a rifle
in case I'm late. Arroyos tumble more calves
than coyotes, cavorting on legs in the air
like a ballet of goats on stilts. Prairie dogs bark
when I ride by, upright by their burrows. Far off,
a coyote's loping somewhere in a hurry, ears back
as if he thinks I'm riding guard for dogs.

Before I'm back with the calf or not,
that coyote will be sleeping it off
in shadows under roots, thinking he's tricked me
again, tricked them all, the squealing rodents
tasty as hot dogs without buns. Over the plains,
the bright sun burns, and soon it will be dark.

The Winter Our Grandson Turned Thirteen

When I open both fists wide, my God!
what wrinkles, like a pond rippled
on a windy day, seen from a thousand feet
in a chopper. Squeezed into fists again,
the skin tries to lie about my age,
betrayed by creases like canals on Mars.

I've seen these hands on Grandfather
in the hospital, an IV needle
taped like a tire patch, my hero
who carved hawks and robins from blocks
of mahogany and oak, feathers so real
I swore he could make the buffed wood fly.

How fast my skimpy lifeline aged
in these palms, old knuckles broken
and stiff. This thumb can't flex
without snapping, bone on bone,
a clicker for Halloween. So this
is how we hold autumn in our hands.

Held wide, the fingers tremble, the fist
I pitched with, that held the stick
in Air Force jets, that slipped the ring
on my wife's finger, fists that held
three babies up to the world as if to beg
Be good, be careful with these kids.

After the Children Leave

The door slams back, back, and glass shatters.
In gusty winds this wild, hawks hunker down like ducks.
Elk thrust noses downhill into trees for a windbreak,
fold gawky all the way down. Burning off snow
like a tongue, wind from the west whips the pines
like ironweeds flicked to loosen dirt from roots.

Too late to fix the lock, I'll nail the door
to keep it shut. When we found this mountain cabin
ten miles from town, we bought it from Somebody Jones' estate,
bachelor without a cousin, without an heir.
He built this stone-walled shack to last, horseshoe
not nailed but bolted above the door. And now

the cabin's ours, magnolia panels and oak
hauled down from Montana. Tomorrow, we'll fix the door,
prop up the chimney with mortar and marble,
call our children in steamy Houston and say come home,
bring grandbabies to breathe this heady air, to see the deer
and marmots, the moss-tall tundra in the clouds.

At Dawn with the Blinds Raised

How does faith come—like a hummingbird darting by,
or a pair of elk cows clipping our grass at dawn,
sniffing the picnic table while we wait
with the blinds raised. Soon, beams will splash
the mountain peak, lights will come on,

a cabin door will close, the elk will lift their heads
and stare, and trot with eyes wide, back to the tree line.
Suddenly, others come, almost glowing in their blond,
thick, winter coats, bowing to grass we've watered
and not mowed, hoping for this moment—four,

fourteen, the whole herd here on our lawn,
sisters and mothers on our green slope,
cougars and coyotes a thousand yards behind them,
calves on their way within weeks—but all that's later,
and the best grass since last summer is right now.

The Midas Touch in Texas

I never needed much, a Midas touch,
a mile-wide ranch of Angus, a sky of geese
and rain clouds, a lovely woman who nibbles my ear
and then says *Please, hubby, love me.*
I've flown to Saigon and back, shot thousands of geese
on the flyway with cameras and prayed for rain,

hardscrabble dirt like rocks. We sank all we own
in babies, gave them their names and blessed them
as each left home. They gave back grandbabies we adore,
who gave us names, *Mamaw* and *Pop.* Nights,
we rock on the back porch, watching stars.
I'm stunned that a woman can be this lovely

at sixty. I thought old women and men
were only old. I see her eyes, the shadows
of her face, thin flecks of silver in her hair.
It hasn't rained in months, but I'm healed
wholly by her touch, amazed each time
she lifts my gnarled, stiff knuckles to her lips.

Batting Practice at Sixty

I slap five dozen balls back through the box,
grounders that hop to the shortstop's glove,
some sneaking through for singles, but not far.
Lately, I've gotten good at fly balls and pop-ups,
swinging too late, cutting under, eye
on the ball but jerking, forcing the bat.
My turn to chase somebody's flies,
so I trot to third and flip the padded hat,

hoping for grounders, ready to scoop
and throw out my arm across the mound
to first. Old folks desperate to improve
should practice twice a day to confound
our sons, not once a week for summer games
in the senior league. I taught my children
to bunt and run, hang tough and hit away
when the sign was right, and slide, be men,

shake hands and come out fighting. But those were days
before Saigon, before our parents died,
back when flying was an easy escape
for me on weekends, before our son's long nights
in Desert Storm, when hopes turned back to fear:
sixty, closets stacked with keepsakes,
videos we watch when the boys are here.
Those snapshots after the game of us
seem ancient, a honeymoon album,

back when Whitey Ford controlled the mound,
Berra behind the plate, a kid in center field
named Mickey Mantle shagging every out,
trying to match Joe DiMaggio's career
in Yankee Stadium, Babe Ruth's bambino face
on the plaque behind him—our fingers curled,
tingling, holding hands, magic and grace
in every field we looked, the whole wide world
before us, the Yankees in first place.

TWO

When Rockets Fell
like Stars

That night, that year
Of now done darkness I wretch lay wrestling with (my God!)
   my God.

—Gerard Manley Hopkins, "Carrion Comfort"

Swaggering to the Flight Line

Out of cram sessions in the bar,
we practiced crashing after midnight,
emergency steps we drilled
until we could fly blindfolded,
stumbling up stairs of the barracks.
We turned unnatural acts around
in our minds, spins and loops

we would have to do perfect,
alone. Out of bachelor bunks,
out of accident reports and training films,
we swaggered to the flight line,
living on flames in the belly of jets,
five thousand pounds of thrust.
Wings and three good friends

sustained us, men we would die for,
table mates straining to take
the IP's brain and luck
and make them ours, aping his stride,
the cock of his flight cap. No coach
ever drove us like that brash
instructor pilot, almost a god,

a man with wings and battle ribbons
and touch on controls we coveted.
One by one he launched us solo
in December skies he owned, cold wind
whipping the ramp when I strapped in
and taxied out without his breath
in my headset—exciting silence,

nothing but these two fists to save me,
the runway thudding faster and faster
and falling away, the moon floating up
from Savannah, the force in my hand massive,
banking with blazing power out of traffic,
climbing through baffling darkness
into the splendor of stars.

Marching through Georgia

We punched holes in Georgia skies
and buried our lust in loops
and lazy-eights, welding ourselves
to forces we'd never known—hard turns

and rolls, spins and Immelmanns
inverted in jets, blinded when blood
flooded our heads like sex. Sundays,
we raided Moultrie, hoping for local girls

lovely as centerfolds pinned to our lockers.
We cruised Georgia nights in Corvettes,
searching for schoolmarms or farm girls
wild to couple with anything with wings.

Mondays, cramped in crash helmets,
we burned from instructors' curses
teaching us touch and trim, how to hold
a ten-ton plane inches away

from wing tips in bumpy air in dives,
how to tighten our guts and come level,
how to climb in combat formation
and if we had to, how to die.

Cousin Eddie and the Jungle Trails

His grip was vicious even at sixteen, four knuckles broken
when he tumbled from a cliff, backpacking with the Scouts,
learning to climb. The iron he pumped bulged muscles
for his age, jaw muscles tight like his heroes.

One of us cousins would fly, the other a Green Beret,
balding first-sergeant sent early to Saigon to save them.
His hard-as-nails advice exploded, torched by faces
of monks burning in the streets. Up jungle trails

he carried the gospel of war to Montagnards,
a man who believed M-16s could save them.
Before body bags and bombing, before any but his platoon
knew he was there, he did his job, walked softly

on jungles paths already flanked by mines,
an adviser lugging no weapons, only his fists,
teaching all he was taught. Years before the build-up,
they shipped him back to Texas in a box.

When Rockets Fell like Stars

We prowled that part of the base at midnight,
high on crowbars and beer. We smashed car lights
and ripped the chrome off doors. Nothing beat
being drunk enough to die when bar girls screamed
and rockets fell like stars, one more
Cadillac dismantled upside down. We swore
whoever owned such cars were black-market heads
or Vietcong cousins who wanted us dead,
boys whose war crashed down in darkness, the rage
of VC mortars and rockets fired at the base.

When I was ten, we met each other's boasts
with knives, how near we could throw at toes
without flinching. One time I pitched too close,
and Joe Bob cursed and hurled the knife at me.
From then on, blades stayed closed and in our jeans.
Talk turned to girls and what to do
if we made somebody bleed. Roaring tunes
with country and western words in Saigon,
trying to ignore all falling fire, we staggered
back to sandbagged bunkers, daring the blare
of sirens to kill us, swearing we didn't care.

Wings Tumbling like a Torch

I didn't see the smoke,
just broke formation as he told me,
pitched steep and felt the blast.
I thought my turbines exploded,

slammed down like a violent storm.
I bounced and rolled toward the sun,
glanced back at Parker's jet on fire,
wings tumbling like a torch.

I dived to follow him down, spiraling
to hold him, to open his back pack
with a vortex, or wake him from the dead.
Get out! I called, *Get out!*—fire and smoke,

and Parker falling. Bits of metal
sprayed like a sparkler, Parker
welded to wreckage or vaporized,
his blood like a mist.

Explosions happen often in ghost stories
at the bar. Sometimes nothing can save us
from fire, bad weather,
or combat. What could I do

when Parker called to warn me,
leaving two sons and a wife,
leaving his call sign to haunt me?
If fire had splashed in my mask,

would I have spent last seconds
to save him, shouting orders
to break steep away, no time
to call to God before the blast?

Gigging for Frogs before the War

I thought about that night while choppers roared.
Lucinda's cousin scoffed, *You call this fun?*
We lay on cots stretched tight between two boards.

We waded mud and left the girls on shore.
We gigged the frogs and strung them one by one.
I thought about that night when choppers roared.

We squished them on a chain between the bones.
What was her name? She cried, *You call this fun?*
We lay on cots stretched tight between two boards.

We held them close and swore we'd let them go,
frogs caught on chains stretched tight to cook till done.
I thought about that night when choppers roared.

What did we know, boys who rode bulls in rodeos?
We kissed both lovely girls and kept frogs strung.
We lay on cots stretched tight between two boards.

Then mortars hit, and grown men flinched and swore.
We cursed dirt bunkers and waited for the sun.
I thought about that night while choppers roared,
alone on a cot stretched tight between two boards.

Bogeyman, 1969

He watched me at night outside Saigon,
demon under my bunk, when God seemed farther
than the dimmest star—him, the enemy,
cast out by God like lightning,
lost in eternal darkness. On my bunk,
I listened hard and heard far in the distance
hospital choppers thudding fast,

gunfire a mile away, the wail of sirens
for incoming rockets. And sometimes, oddly,
silence—only the thump of concussions,
someone's hard-rock tape in the barracks
bluffing the bogeyman back where he belonged,
crushed under decks of cards and *Playboys*.
I heard someone's breath in my bunk,

mine, mine. I never wondered if hell
was a bluff. I felt I would die in a flash,
the twinkling of an eye, and why not,
rockets had to crash somewhere.
I groveled in dreams toward God. Always
he was there when I least expected—not God
but the demon, no matter how many laps

I jogged around the track, how many tasks
I wrapped up tight for the Colonel,
how many hours in the command post
I studied Plexiglas battle maps,
the Cong's advances lit by twinkling lights.
I saw no exit, caught like Custer's men
hip-deep in prairie grass in a battle

already lost. We were alone in jungles
on a globe floating in the dark
eternal mystery of space, red lights
winking at Saigon on the map, the demon
laughing behind the glass. Battalions
rode from the north armed with rockets,
our only hope to charge, to kill them all.

But It Was Water

Riding dry fields, men carry canteens
wherever they go, the only water hole
the mud they can dig in creeks of caliche,
the only shade their Stetsons,
the only rain clouds rumors.

Years ago, training to survive a war
no one I cared for wanted,
we dug in a western desert,
caught a rattler coiled beside brown water.
Gosheff faked the rattler with his fist

and the snake hissed back and fell,
splashing as if it meant to die there,
not up on the dirt where we wanted.
It churned our pool to venom.
With sticks we dipped it out

and killed it. We found a rusted pot
and boiled it, muddy, but it was water,
so we dipped and drank it all.
Now, on fields I share with goats
and rattlers, after the rain and jungles

of Saigon, I ride alone and wonder
how much poison we swallowed,
how many miles to the cabin,
how many times a good horse
stumbles over stones.

Beside the Dark-Sheened Water

The stock of Father's shotgun on my cheek
flashed lightning at clouds no thicker than topsoil
dry as a tongue. Always we killed our limit,
though who could count, my brother and me just boys.
I believed wings could save me and flew home
to those plains after Saigon. Our father
left us all he had, and there we were once more
carving our names in clouds with shotguns.

They boomed and ricocheted, the only sounds,
though somehow that was enough. We picked up
doves like manna, the one scarce crop. We found
a round stock tank with algae sides and plucked
the soft gray feathers, the dark-sheened water
bulging. Even the dunking of doves made it surge
and gush, overflowing to sand. Swished under,
the plucked dove breasts came clean, emerged
cold and glistening, dark as hearts. Lead pipes
of windmill towers turned all the west could shove
to water. Always, buzzards soared, a wild
hosanna of meat. Hunting after a war for doves,

I hear something say *Be still.* Packs of wild dogs
roam the plains, angels with fangs and fleas.
Overseas, dogs trotted behind me like Gog
and Magog, Armageddon beasts in the heat
and fear of battle, panting. Jungles begged
to be spared, the trapped mind desperate to live,
though there was no way back to the simple dregs
of childhood, never to believe the myth
those jolly fat men's beards were real, toys
built by elves, not bought by parents who don't
age gracefully, but moan like dying boys
and disappear like gods or fairy ghosts

with fetishes for sleep. The mind has a spine
like a tap root, survives blunt sun and thunder,
even when last great lies explode. At all times
everything takes luck, even that buzzard
gliding above us, hatched with only one thing
to do—but ah, what hard incisive eyes
and instinct, what dark outrageous wings.

That Silence When
a Mountain Lion Attacks

Those puffy clouds in the Rocky Mountains
could be gunfire, another time and place.
Before this planet spins us back home to the plains,
dozens will die by rockets or cannon fire,

puffs like clouds the last skies they will see.
I heard explosions often in Saigon
and the rapid pop of rifles, but high over jungles
I saw only distant puffs and fire, silence

except my own breath and chatter in my headset.
Even when Kelly exploded in mid-air, no others heard,
only a blip that disappeared on radar screens
back at Da Nang. The earth turns green again,

no matter what. Outside our cabin, magpies clown
and crazy hop for worms and lazy bugs, sluggish
under a thawing, Colorado sun. Last week,
two campers had their throats slit in their tent

not ten miles east. We never heard a scream.
The world will be the world, springtime or not.
Our oldest daughter's forty and a day, and we are wiser
only by repute. The cost of living past a war

bankrupts the heart. Feelings are cash stashed in cigar boxes
and not invested, no access by the Internet.
Only an elk calf knows how its neck feels
pierced by a puma, how nothing matters when fangs

bend it staggering back, unable to scream
or breathe. Others don't need to know, but if they could,
they'd trade—nobody's pain has been shared
anywhere, no other's loss is ever this severe.

To the Tribe

I believe in jerks
who throw fast food together,
who pop the corn
for horror shows,
who pump the gas. At eight,
I walked back after work
splattered with paint,
breathing the smoke
of buses, saving my dime
for a Hershey halfway home.
Outside Saigon
I sweated in jungle boots
and trudged with buddies,
all of us jerks
who wanted only
the love of someone
and the grace of breath.

For Friends Missing in Action

When I take my meddling friend for coffee,
he picks at paper napkins, shredding lint
like snow. Before Mary Jane pours refills,
Joe asks how long I've been up, how many

empty beer cans I've recycled, how many
crows and skunks I've shot. He knows whose daughters
are overdue, whose son's gone overseas.
Squeezing his mug, he gripes about lawyers,

tells me which older widows he's seeing,
which of the younger have money, which ones
seem faithful to their holy ghosts. Like this
week by week, even when other buddies

drop by, the booth full of elbows, aisle blocked
by extra chairs. Only Earl smokes, ash trays
banished. Earl paces in the parking lot,
puffing, staring at nothing. Joe asks Ray

about Earl's work, his jitters and weight loss.
Ray only frowns, and Joe falls back and sighs.
I read Joe's whispers as signs, those folded arms
as a warning. When Earl returns, I catch his eye,

and Earl stares back and nods, as if he's seen
the clues I saw, bamboo nicked by a flicked
machete, the oozing stalks and swarms of bees.
Flicking his eyes between us, scooping the lint

and squeezing, Joe leans close. *What's up?* he pumps.
He stares past us at something far away,
angry if one of us says *Nothing* or only shrugs.
Nothing we could say would be enough today.

THREE

Wishing for Friends from Childhood

Not breathing "Father,"
At Nimblewill,
But saying, "Fathers! Fathers!"

—James Dickey, "Hunting Civil War Relics
at Nimblewill Creek"

The Summer Her Family
Moved to Houston

Don't ask, Uncle Bill scolded.
You don't want to know. Oh, but I did,
Aunt Emma bursting with secrets
I should know. What happens when a body rots,

when cancer eats the lungs? What did he mean,
exquisite pain? Nine, I had felt fire
when I swallowed with my tonsils gone—
saved by a fire brigade of nurses

with ice cream. I had seen dead pigs,
found my brother's old dog stiff
behind the barn. What could be worse
than watching Barbara ride off

in her family's packed station wagon,
waving from the tailgate and weeping,
leaving for Houston a thousand miles away?
Oh, if anything would ever be worse

than watching their vacant house for hours
across the road, no one to ride with
across a mile of meadow to the muddy Brazos,
Barbara forever gone, I had to know.

Barter

A blue-healer pup nuzzling my toes
meant more than silver dollars. *Saucy,*
I called her, hard for Uncle Ray to show
four dozen pups a year and name each
before weaning, sold to hunters who drove
all night for his hounds. All summer,
I churned Aunt Edna's butter, dug post holes,
milked the herd. One dawn, milk sloshed over

on my feet, and one fat puppy lapped my toes.
I put both buckets down and picked her up.
Her tongue wouldn't stop, popping as she poked
and licked, tail like a wind-up pup's.
Daily she followed while I squeezed the teats,
missing the bucket on purpose, the stream
hissing on my feet, then back with a thump
in the bucket. Saucy washed my dusty feet

in the barn and all the dawdling way
to the house. I confess, Uncle Ray
warned me, each pup worth more than my pay—
the best hunting season in years. I swore
I'd work free until Christmas, skip school,
weed his fallow pastures and pick the grapes,
but that fat litter sold in June.

Chocolate

My own behavior baffles me.
　　　　　　　—Romans 7:15

One night, my father let the screen door slam
and shined a lantern at the barn and trees
around the yard, the fierce red eyes of cats
caught shining in the light. They stared
then slipped away. My angry father stopped,
arcing the beam like a switchblade.
Through the floor of my tree fort, I watched.
It sliced through cracks by my face,
blazing on branches. I didn't breathe.
Then I was alone again in that dark place,

peeling and trembling, eating the last, sweet
Hershey bar. My father's bobbing beam
stabbed the pump house, the tractor.
He stopped at the barn, massive, supreme,
the master, and me the outcast, the bastard.
He barked my name again and waited.
Munching, I watched him in the dark. Chocolate
coiled oily around my mouth like a snake.
Oh, I loved chocolate, just one small bar
each month before my sister's birthday—

41

our parents' gift, those brown and silver bars
in a box with see-through cellophane,
and all for her. My father laid the flashlight
to his thigh, like a white-hot branding iron.
His big leg glowed as if burning. Nowhere to hide,
I crawled to the edge to breathe, on fire
with fear, hiding my face. My eyes watered
and chocolate bubbled in my gut,
a tub of trouble and me with chocolate
greasy on my lips, about to heave. Still, I sucked

the gummy fudge as if starving. Looking back,
I can't explain why I swallowed and licked
the sticky mess, peeled each crisp paper back
and cleaned each waxy crease, licking my lips
and fingers, gorged and sweating, almost sick.
But my tongue still flicked at slivers so small
they were tasteless, a snake's tongue flicking,
flicking even at crumbs. I ate them all.
I must have gone inside at dawn, been whipped
or sent to bed without supper—if so,

what grace. My sister forgave, or let me live.
Maybe I bought her caramels or French cologne,
hoping to mend Humpty Dumpty with glue.
I don't know why I still like chocolate,
or why we moved. But after that night, I knew
where Eden was—that ranch before the war.
Even now, I still see Father's flashlight
swinging from pump house to tractor for me,
crawling, starting to beg for help that night
in whispers, sweet wrappers littered at my feet.

Grandfathers

Grandpa Dees hauled explosives in World War Two
until the accident. My mother taught me not to cheer
when John Wayne saved the wagon train, Grandpa
one of *them*. But I thought tall John Wayne
was god, what the awesome white man in the sky
would look like, if he shaved. I saved my dimes

and went to movies, anyway, silent in the crowd,
slumped down and gobbling popcorn,
believing every scene. My uncles swore by boots
and cowboy hats, sons of my other grandpa.
In town and family picnics, they scowled
and swaggered like the Duke, hats tilted down

over dark eyebrows, wrists cocked
at belt level, drawling, talking softly.
I saw how funny it all was at thirteen. Grandpa Dees
wore sneakers and a baseball cap, hauled explosives
in an eighteen-wheeler all through the war.
Back for a night, Grandpa tangled me in headlocks,

rubbed my flattop raw with flint-rock knuckles,
dumped me on my back and raised a hatchet
or a souvenir dog from Arkansas
or California, giving me candy canes,
an eagle's feather, then lifted and hugged me
tight as a son until his truck pulled out.

Growing Up by the Brazos

In caves hacked out by tomahawks
we traded knives and arrowheads,
pieces of pottery and bones.
That deep in the country

no teachers prowled, no little brothers
tagging along and crying after dark.
White caliche crumbled when we dug.
We swatted cobwebs, hoping for treasure

buried by tribes a thousand years ago,
shovels of gold inches away. Now,
nothing tumbles down this canyon
but scorpions and coyotes

starving for the moon.
Years before diggers uncovered skulls
of buffalos and wolves, we believed
this canyon on the plains hid ghosts.

Huddled around fires, spitting
bitter tobacco, we held up bones
and argued what they were, coyote
or human. We told the old lies

faithfully after dark—the one
about the maiden nobody found,
the ghost looking for his bloody arm,
the slaughtered wagon train.

Tatters of ghosts and smoke
clung to us all night long,
sockets of dry skulls hollow
and wild tongues strangely close.

Grandmother Bankhead's Lake

Sprawled on our bellies, we clawed through muck
and Irish potatoes under Grandmother Bankhead's house
on stilts. We turned the loam with pitchforks,

lifting fat worms writhing on tines. Copperheads
lived there, and waterdogs, black widow spiders.
I felt them crawl, and slapped, smacking my skull.

My cousin hissed *Shut up!* as if worms had ears.
Our great-grandfather dammed that pond in the Civil War,
birthright for boys with fishing rods and bait,

the coolest shade in Alabama. Later that month,
one uncle died on the beach of Okinawa,
the last big battle of the war. But now, bass and catfish

waited for our worms, graves of uncles in magnolia groves,
their oddly familiar names on plaques. Bodies of boys
and horses had washed down to the dam, steel markers said.

Wading to cast past tangled vines and mosquitoes,
I imagined corpses bobbing in the spring-fed lake,
bloody skulls and ribs nibbled by fish along the bank.

Boys and Their Fathers' Shotguns

Carl hugged the gun
he sneaked from his father,
shaking his head and sobbing.
What madness made him whirl
and shoot both barrels

at Billy Ray, what angel
shoved Billy's head
a second before the blast?
Squinting, Billy Ray sprawled,
head cocked as if seeing visions.

Carl offered the shotgun
with both hands, begged Billy Ray
to take it, shoot it all day,
but please don't tell.
Billy Ray held his head,

still on his knees between cactus
as if looking for contacts.
Carl's crotch and eyes darkened,
the stain spreading wide
on his Levis. We didn't laugh,

not even when Carl tried to hide it,
the shotgun trembling in his fists,
thunder we'd carry forever
more dangerous than snakes,
the cold blue metal of barrels.

Uncle Croom's Attic

He had the only pin-ball machine not rigged
and let us flip until our fingers ached.
We worshipped him for that and beer
he let us sip. I thought he was only lazy,
staying drunk while Aunt Sandra tended the sick.

Aunt Sandra smashed all bottles he brought in
when she was off cleaning someone's sores
in the rest home. One day in the attic
we found his uniform, his purple heart and sword.
We'd seen rolled posters of stiff Marines,

square-jawed, razor sharp, not at all like Croom
sprawled in pajamas, holding an Atlas and scratching,
the fireplace cold where he sat watching for Sandra,
books about the world war scattered, hair matted
as if he'd been in a storm all afternoon.

As Time Goes By

I'm losing the limp, blue taste of her kiss,
the over and under roll of her body in water.
When we kicked and rose to breathe, rockets hissed
far from the starlit lake, firecrackers popped,
the whole town watching, grass and bleachers packed.
We bobbed in water like waltzing, bumping thighs
and hips and toes, treading water, watching the backs
of their heads, the flash and sizzle of rockets rising

above the crowd to burst, scattering flowers
of sparks over all the park, reds and greens
fizzing out and down, white phosphorus showers
over *ohhs* and *ahhs* of families. Sixteen,
sticky in the heat of July, we had left the swings
and slides behind and raced to the lake, too dark
to be missed, tugging off clothes, wading the slick
beach mud. Diving, we swam to the buoy like an ark,

bobbing, trying to breathe while we kissed.
If only her father had died in the war
or retired and come back, she might not have missed
her senior year, bobbing so far from the shore,
Korea calling all boys to war like her father.
He called his family to Tokyo, and she was gone
by August—the empty house, her parakeet and dogs,
the park's Fourth of July fireworks and lawn

cleaned long ago, the hard half-eaten hot dog buns
tossed to the ducks. Long letters came for months,
wide rows of kisses, a hint of Japanese perfume
scrolling down and around each border, a blue
fire-breathing dragon at the top of each gold page,
flames from its tongue more vivid than her face.

Grandfather and the Boys
He Knew in School

Old men whittled oak for hours.
Grandfather led them, *flick,* and *flick,*
and old friends followed like a rhythm band.
Down on the county square, on benches of iron bars
straddling fat roots of elms and hemlock,

decades before the high-rise jail or seniors' center,
the spit-and-whittle club punched the clock
like bankers' hours, nowhere to go but home—
a Dodge sedan with the seat down, or a shack.
Earl and I played jackknife with those men,

mumbletypeg, blackjack for matches. One by one
we watched them cough into bloody handkerchiefs and die
or disappear, praising God or Roosevelt one day,
then gone. One year, I found park benches empty,
nothing but squirrels on the county square,

and most of those looked old, hobbling like dogs
on all fours, not hopping. Never mind
that some old men wheezed *Help,* strapped down
in nursing homes like Grandfather, fed by college boys
like me, to pay tuition. Sometimes I see arms

around bars of the ten-story county jail
where the courthouse was, where squirrels
and toddlers had roamed, where old men wailed
about the drought and taxes and shook stiff knuckles
at each other, their only remaining friends.

First Solo in Thunder

I bounced like a ball
on swept wings bending
and bucking. I believed in gyros
and dials, and ignored vertigo
that swore I was falling.

Boots firm on the rudders,
I rode the rotors
through valleys of lightning,
trusting the ratio of stress,
the azimuth of fire.

Slamming through downdrafts,
I broke into sunlight, on course
and almost home. Boys playing ball
may have glanced at a roar
far away, heads back and scanning.

Old men who had seen it all
maybe stared, hands raised,
watching for whatever's there,
stunned by a glimpse of silver
beyond sound.

Instant Replay

Staying home was easy
after the pulling guard
faked me wide
twice before half,
and the tailback cut back
and cleated the grass
I bulldozed with my nose.

I never forgot to hold my breath,
not even the first time
my father tossed me
off the deep end, *Sink
or swim,* he barked, and I sank
into his will and stayed at home,
a loyal son to my father,

who proved one night
history doesn't always repeat—
dying, he stiff-armed the tackler
and dashed around end
out of bounds,
up through the stands
and over the distant hills.

The Last Pullman to Houston

Sometimes we see them when we're back
hiking to the pond, spikes rusted dark,
the color of smoke, in this silence
since the last train rolled away to Houston

years ago. No whistle, no flattened pennies
on the rails, no roar or rattling windows.
Old Uncle Bubba claims he waved
at the Duke of Windsor's private car one year,

three movie stars whose films I never saw,
a hundred Pullman cars a week.
The tracks are gone, the crossties
buried under sand. It curved here

where the weeds are high. One year
digging for spikes, we filled four buckets
and waddled home. We lined them up
by size, the shape of their points,

how bright we could shine them
on Grandfather's grind wheel
in the barn, and hung them
like silver ingots on the wall.

Wishing for Friends
from Childhood

Muscles bulged under our tank tops,
goofy boys with hair slicked back with oil.
Bobby Sollis and I were tall and tan.
The algebra teacher teased we were bad
but made us her pets. Our hot breaths
puffed her blouse when, over our desks,
she taught dumb Milly how to add.
We carved our names in girlfriends' homes
but never climbed the tower, not bold
like Edward, who fell, crushing his skull.
We weren't foolhardy like Durwood, who stole
and ran before cops came with handcuffs.

We played football, broke our fists
and ribs and swaggered in letter jackets.
In '50, Bobby begged me to enlist.
Bobby died in spite of a flak jacket
and Plexiglas, his bomber shot down,
his tail gun blazing. Two decades later,
the world was Vietnam, jungles I went to
middle-aged, crazy to be in bamboo
and monsoon, a war fought by boys the age
of Bobby Sollis when he and I rode Harleys,

the flash of rockets like sermons I hated
about hell, where maybe Durwood was, snarly,
afraid of nothing. I saw them all
in the sweat and blink of my rage,
friends bloody or huddled in bunkers,
and felt nothing could save us, not Durwood
or God or Bobby Sollis, nothing at all.

Facing It

I suppose you turn on the horizon,
expecting me, both of you on tiptoe,
others bumping past like pilgrims.
That time when I was five at the Royal Gorge
comes back to haunt me, wandering off
across that swaying bridge a thousand feet
over the fast, white-water Arkansas.

While my father checked the oil and water
and Mother spread sandwiches in the shade
and made my brothers help, I leaned
and spat at that deep drop-off,
watched the white foam arc and shine
until gone. Cars chugged behind me, old cars
that would have to last four years more

during World War II. *Don't fall,*
some mother called, and I heard my mother
also calling *Walt, don't fall!*
from back on the canyon rim, helpless
as if afraid her weight might snap the cables
with me precarious and trapped.
Two decades later, I banked an Air Force jet

at 20,000' and snapped the camera at that bridge
an inch long at arm's length to show you
it was nothing. I held the wingtips vertical,
spiraled down to 500' above the crowd,
nudged the throttle and climbed
until the bridge was an inch, a quarter inch.
I hummed and held ten thousand pounds of power

in my fist. I flew to Saigon a decade later
and came back to the scramble of surviving,
to children running and tumbling
over dangerous bridges I'd never crossed,
and to my aging father and mother almost gone,
the drawbridge rising while I stood
helpless and waving a few yards away.

FOUR

Search and Rescue

In Israel, in order to be a realist you must believe in miracles.

—David Ben-Gurion

Diamonds in the Carnegie Museum

Our guide was blind and kind, chatting about diamonds
we half circled like a wagon train in a box canyon,
no way out but united for the night,
bound for Montana. She was thirty-five or forty,
without a ring. Her dazzling eyes rolled back

and blinked. She was singing, prattling
about diamond mines and dreams, but singing,
her voice charming us to look. She loved those halls
she never saw, loved all of us she had touched
in the lobby, touched each one only once

but knew us, or made us believe she did.
I wondered what marvels she could sing about
or show. She turned and tapped her way
with a penlight-thin retractable pole,
turned to the bulletproof transparent glass

and sighed. She was a bride among diamonds
and we mere cousins in from the cold, lucky to share
what she held at arm's length every day,
too precious to wear, crushed coal and fire
in the heart of earth too radiant to see.

The Songs
of Country Girls

Who are these singers with sequined eyes
and paste-on nasal twangs? Wild horses
couldn't make these girls look plain.
They pinch the mikes with scarlet nails,
balancing diamond rings like birds.
Bring back the days of faithful girls

so homely they hurt. They moaned old songs
in smoky halls, strong-jawed women
choking back real tears. Where are they,
now that we need them? When their hearts broke,
we swayed and held them close, humming softly
to ourselves and waltzing to the grave.

Bull-Necked and Square-Jawed after Saigon

I'm a pawn of dawn on the plains, of sentimental rhymes
Sinatra sang, even awkward magicians' tricks.
Weep me a Lloyd Webber cello and I'll weep,
glass-jawed and masked like a monster at a concert.
Let soprano choir boys in Vienna hit a high note,

let my grandson's teacher lead him
and other gawky boys in nasal cowboy songs—
it doesn't matter—I'm the bull-necked grandfather I am,
reaching for Kleenex, about to bawl. My cowboy father
fought in Flanders, but after his stroke

he choked back pity at wrestling matches
and game shows on TV, maudlin old man
cracking knuckles of both his massive fists.
Lucky man with allergies, I'm forgiven this Texas nose
I blow, red eyes I wipe as if I'm crying.

Where did this awful heart come from, unless from him,
marbled like a slab of prime rib, bloody chunk
plopped on the plate with new potatoes and peas?
I came back from Saigon vulnerable at any black wall
in Washington, a ticking time bomb that explodes

when I'm walking along in Lubbock or London
and come upon someone down on a sidewalk,
chalking a gaudy mauve-and-purple pop art,
and I stumble by like a blind man, blinking as if sand
or smog in my contacts is scratching my eyeballs raw.

My Father and the Sad Soap Operas

Don't cry, my daddy said, slapping that razor strap.
How that man could hold and hit. His father taught him respect
with a belt and the back of his hand. For years, I thought God
gave him that arm, no fistfights like Daddy's calm-faced licks.
I wished I'd find him someday in a wheelchair, maybe by a lake,
tumbling in with a fishing pole, no one but me to save him.

After Vietnam, I found him already healed, clumsy the ways
he tried to hide his passion for soap operas, crossing his feet
on the lounger, squeezing back screams and trembling,
blowing his nose. I'll never know what happened
while I was gone—maybe his first grandchild, my mother's cancer,
his own first stroke that flipped him to the floor.

I've seen that look on others—tears for dogs run over—
but never saw my dad cast down by demons like a man.
I wondered what to do—scowl or walk away, switch channels
or slip outside for a smoke. I thought of fields where he fought
in Flanders, the body bags and burning huts I saw around Saigon,
and held that man and held him while he shook.

All Dogs Are Pirates

All dogs are pirates, wild for an opened gate,
a different scent. At any jiggled leash,
Old Rollo stumbled to the door, begging
for plunder, wagging his bulldog butt.

I've seen dogs try to board others, sniffing,
tails up like flags, or down on their backs
like sailors giving up. Dogs in Montana
tug their tourists uphill at Little Bighorn,

sniffing for clues, gobbling pretzels and bread
tossed for the crows, peeing on signs with fines
for stealing bones. Dogs rock the boat
of good manners, barking at startled guests

on the porch, probing with noses like hooks,
lifting up purses and skirts for inspection,
scratching, licking themselves before we cast them
adrift in the back yard black as a dungeon.

Armadas of dogs sail by, marking the alley fence
like treasure maps, to make them bark. Guests gone,
dogs lope inside and sniff the floor for gold
before bedtime, panting, holding no grudge.

For years, Old Rollo drooled and groaned
by our chairs, happy with any tidbit
we tossed, fat belly scratched until his leg
thumped, any pat like a ration of rum.

Hardscrabble, Tooth and Claw

Prairie dogs leap and fall, tumbling off mounds
and scampering. Hawks patrol blue skies,
hunters roaming the plains where thin clouds
puff and disappear. Wind brings lullabies
and love songs to the pups. Older dogs bark
warnings, fat furry rodents upright
like kangaroos. Their world is sand and rocks,
the cactus of plains forever dry.

Deep burrows trip fat cattle, legs snapped,
proving how little dirt is tame. Hawks glide
for hours down valleys of burrs and cactus,
tracking pups that bark at silent skies,
baffled by fire of fierce claws piercing
their backs, the sudden flapping of wings.

Abandoned Shack in Bankhead National Forest

Carl McDonald in 1840 hammered the last rough plank
back into place, lay down with his wife for years
and died. This could be the home, these broken boards
splintered at the end like brooms, this abandoned,

hand-built family house that never burned
though most of northern Alabama blazed.
When Carl McDonald died, did family come
from miles around in wagons?—most cousins dead

or buried back in rocky Scotland.
Great-great-grandmother Martha dug the loam
and lowered him herself, God of her fathers harsh
but provident, and somehow she survived.

That fall, she bore my great-grandfather,
wounded in the war when he was sixteen,
too poor to own a farm, to even vote,
his wound a legacy to all McDonald men,

stiff-shouldered in the cold. Now, here it is,
a shack almost collapsed, bound by kudzu
tight as baling wire. Sniff the vinegar-sweet sap
bubbling out of Alabama pine. Hear the whack

of Carl McDonald's axe, the idiot joy
of mockingbirds like the clang of metal ladles
as Martha McDonald from Scotland
stirred a pot of soup outside and sang.

Search and Rescue
in the Mountains

Slopes with elk and sheep fall below us
when we climb over tundra past the snow
onto cliffs that mean no harm to climbers
or even mountain goats that fall,
or jet aircraft that crash.

We believe help is there sometimes
when we need it, though some days
nothing can save us. Even Jesus
who could cast mountains into seas
knew what little time we have.

If we never pass this way again
what is that to rocks tumbling down
and geese with a thousand miles to fly
back to arctic lakes to breed?
We pound steel pitons into stone

as a last resort and loop the ropes,
insert our boots and step out into space
and swing across slick granite
to a ledge of faith, where there was fire
on the mountain once, nothing now

but seared strips of metal that look
almost like a plane. For hours, we tag
and photograph, and scoop a human
into sacks of plastic that last longer
than blood and breath we cling to

like these ropes that lift us
spinning off the cliff, over chasms
thousands of feet straight down,
nothing above us but one helicopter
throbbing like salvation's heart,

bolts and computer chips put there
by human hands. And dangling here
and spinning above the seared,
sheer granite cliff, we know
we are not angels, not even beasts.

John Parker and
the Captured Mount

His pinto was skittish for weeks, the saddle
unnatural at dawn, spitting the bit,
kicking when the bugler blew attack.
It balked at the feed trough,
tossing its mane. Trooper Parker
rubbed a cavalry blanket under it,
stroking the muzzle, along the legs and back.
It shuddered, but began to munch the grass,
the oats. Now, at Little Bighorn, it drank,
flicking its tail, splashing John Parker's face.

Weeks ago, his best horse lame, when he caught
that Indian pinto miles from the last
Wyoming battle, his bald first sergeant spat
and waved him away. When the pinto balked
at the bugle's blast, the sergeant cursed
him back to the rear, detached and eating dust.
He didn't mind riding drag in Montana,
wiping his neck with a wet bandanna,
last to leave the shallow river, splashing
when the Colonel's yellow hair flashed.
Look at that, John Parker thought, miles of grass

he would die for, wide valley and mountains
white-capped in the west. When the garrison
formed in New York, that's why he joined—a house
of his own, a homestead after his hitch.
He'd pitch a tent by the river—maybe this
wide grassy bank, or there, under those oaks—
until he could make two cattle pay, go home
and find a wife—or there, by those four puffs
of smoke. No horses reared below the bluff
as his did, fighting the bit. *Now*, he thought.
He saw Major Reno's men wheeling off

to guard the flank, the main unit's flag
flapping uphill, another surprise attack.
He nudged the pinto faster, patting its back.
Wherever the Colonel led, John Parker
would follow out of that valley, scared or not,
that yellow hair like federal gold,
sword bouncing at his side. His pinto loped
as though it finally knew what to do,
head bobbing, no matter how many Sioux
painted for war were mounted with lances,
how many pintos pranced, fed by Montana grass.

Reading *Ecclesiastes* at Sixty

My great-greats came to Texas plains
maybe on a dare, hair sticking wildly out
of old men's ears and grannies' bonnets,
prairies so wide no one would hear

if they hollered. They hummed gospel songs
anyway, shoring up dugouts to sleep in.
Their horses were lean and hard jawed,
crunching buffalo grass and dreaming.

Too young to marry, my grandmother
fanned her dying brother in a wagon's shade.
I hear the *swish, swish* of the songbook,
hymnal her family packed down from Ohio.

Her daddy believed God was plain as prairies
after Eden. Settlers needed lakes to bathe,
to dunk their children, each playa lake
a natural baptistery, a tank for their cattle.

Grandpa broke mustangs around the town,
broke both his legs, and the hearts of all three
Johnson girls when he courted Cora Graves.
Wolves killed the sheep that winter,

and two babies died. When dust storms howled
in March, families huddled under gusts
for days, choking, cursing when they heard
their windmills and privies flattened.

When the wind stopped, eight families left,
covered wagons tattered, cattle tethered
and scared. Cora Graves's family stayed,
and so my grandpa stayed.

A Thousand Miles of Stars

I thought I'd need a thousand sweethearts
when I rode bulls in rodeos—and villas in Italy,
Geneva, Tahiti. Palominos pranced
and nudged my fist for sugar cubes, nibbling my palm.
Dogs barked and called me master with their tails,
wagging, dragging my slippers. I fancied leopards
and monkeys doing amazing tricks to please me,
red and blue toucans perched by my chair,

cooing, free to fly in and out, preened and singing
when I came home. Dreams were brahma bulls
after corrals and stirrups, when I was alone under stars
by the bunkhouse. What did I know, straddling a black,
two-thousand-pound bull twisting and bucking,
a thousand fans cheering the cowboy and the bull?
On dance floors with girls with purple eyes
and perfumed, tequila breath, how could I whisper more

than old western words from a jukebox? Now,
at sixty, stiff when I saddle the same fat gelding
I've fed for a decade, I miss our children
who bring their offspring yearly to the ranch,
prizes my wife and I don't stack on the mantle,
but hold to our chests until they leave,
waving goodbye as they drive off at dusk.
When even the dust has settled, we close the gate

and hobble to the porch, old lovers who shake our heads
and laugh, recalling the fall the toddler took
but climbed back giggling to the porch,
how quickly they learned to rope, the giddy
long-distance calls the teenagers made to boys.
We rock and hold each other. We listen hard
and hear dogs bark almost a mile away, the windmill
spinning fast, the far-off roar of stars.

In the Shallow Molasses

In months of harsh sun like a hammer,
our ranch parches like Kalahari summers
after Eden. Hippos snort and waddle off
through dust. Elephants with babies starved
for water and slopping in rotting clay
remember a river miles away
and turn there for salvation. Frog ponds
swallow the sun like salt, and prawns
turn back to clods. Geese sip the last brown sap
and flap, flap to rise. The warthog flounders,
the least beast of creation, half-finished,
formed of the mud of the fields. In pitch

between carrion of monkeys and snakes, the flesh
of half-eaten gazelles, frogs hold their breath,
wedging their skulls deep, deep into holes
until it rains. Here, the lungfish wallows
and thrashes, gills down, thick lips like a bass
gulping air, in the shallow molasses
of mud. Bubbles rise up from the breath hole.
Mud hardens over its mouth, the earth's own throat.
This fish, dried flat as faith, turns stiff,
but if it rains, if it floods, it will live.

Watching Parades
in the Game Room

And though the last lights off the black West went
Oh, morning, at the brown brink eastward, springs—
— Gerard Manley Hopkins, "God's Grandeur"

We didn't know we'd find them in the cemetery,
hobbling arm in arm to the bus stop.
We almost call, although we saw them only at noon,
watching parades on TV in the game room.

Caretakers have dredged the last grave of the day,
rumbled back to the barn and gone home. By now,
those workers have washed their arms and brows,
sat down to beans and cornbread, or maybe steak.

The flags are gone, collected by armloads
for next year's Veterans Day, the local legion post
aging, so many back from Vietnam or Desert Storm
shaking the dust from their boots, not many joining.

Someday, who'll plant the flags? Soon,
my wife's mother and father will enter the hall
of the rest home. She'll help him escape
from his coat, slowly, and lead him to his room.

She'll hang up his hat, and ease him down
into bed. He'll frown as if trying to decide
who is that woman, how long till supper.
She'll smooth those thin white wisps back into place,

part them with fingertips and kiss him.
After supper, after more TV, she'll wave goodnight,
and hug her coat and scarf down the hall to her room,
close enough to hear him, if he calls.

The Risk of Having Children

A nurse works there all night,
but I'm up now, hours before dawn,
away from our grandchild, who cries
and tries to turn. Deer on the lawn
graze quietly. Soon, they'll be gone
across the meadow, as if they might

have been only shadows I believed
were deer. At five, another nurse
will come, tuck in the sheet
and stare, and take her pulse.
Our daughter-in-law will stir,
rise to her elbows to see,

lie back and try to sleep.
Our son is home, drained from his watch,
near the phone, falling asleep,
I hope. If only the pain would stop
when she's awake, the cancer stop,
the clocks jump forward

to news some smocked researcher
shouts on the Internet.
Near my elbow, my computer
waits, the blue screen ready,
the cursor blinking, steady
as monitors in intensive care.

In the dark, I start the coffee,
time for my watch at the hospital.
Sipping, I glance out at the lawn,
red light steady on the fresh-brewed pot.
My wife wakes, drawn by the hot aroma,
the hope and coffee of another dawn.

FIVE

East of Eden

Under new management, Your Majesty: Thine.

—John Berryman, "Eleven Addresses to the Lord"

Killing Nothing but Time

Snakes slither under rich milk cows all day,
hunting mice and lizards, cows and cactus the only shade
for rattlers that thrive on prairies made for drought.
When these are the plains you ride, you bow to the sky

in a hat. Neck and ears burn anyway, skin cancer
bounced from sand to your eyes no matter how wide
the brim. Grandfather taught me to waddle and ride
while Uncle Carl slogged in Pacific swamps, shot dead

on Okinawa. His dog tags dangle from my neck,
my own tags stashed after Vietnam in the attic.
I've fenced these fields so many years I'm brown,
chaps and Stetson my disguise. Often at dawn

I see old neighbors in the distance, other vets
back from the jungles, guns slung low and hats
tugged down. I meet them past the corral, or wait
by the windmill grinding its clatter. I see it in their eyes

sometimes, the way snakes go their own way, alone,
not fearing a man or his rifle. Today, we're giddy
after steaks and biscuits, ready to patch barbed wires
and brand, to break strange colts with words,

easy, easy. Maybe something came back to them
last night, wart-faced and haunting, nothing else
on these wide plains like Vietnam. But here together
we're safe, brave enough in boots and Stetsons, men

of the sunburned eyeballs, riding high over rattlers,
taking turns yelling jokes and shouting with laughter,
twisting and creaking in saddles, killing nothing
but time, riding home to our wives after dark.

Leaving Sixty

A neighbor's cat ambled by, wetting our sand
casually, as natural as lions
in the Kalahari marking their range. That cat
killed a squirrel, sniffing to be sure it died.

We saw her crouched by our porch
in a heap of leaves, not really eating.
Later, I hauled it off, the dumpster loaded
with leaves, dust in the air, spring cleaning,

people sneezing when we walked to the park and back,
cats and squirrels everywhere, the leash law
only for dogs. Now, the drowsy cat
sauntered across the road toward home, yawned,

and leaped to the porch like a baobab tree's
wide bough, lolled like a lion, eyes closed
with one paw dropped, tail flopping,

dreaming of the hunt, of the screaming
panting impala as jaws snatched the throat
for a better hold and squeezed.

After the Random Tornado

Harvest won't save our barn from twisters
on plains flat as the moon. A keg of nails
can't make old rafters safe for owls
and heifers mild as saints. The last tornado

smashed the church a mile away like match sticks,
sinners saved by grace. Lucky for cows,
the twister froze, veered off
and left their calves alone. Our barn's a maze

of tin and splinters, nothing to do but tear it down
and raise one better for bumper crops.
Fat cattle are in our fields, all fences tight,
a pasture of calves all spring.

But watch the stingy cirrus clouds for signs—
buzzards circling the gate, angels prowling
in the shape of funnels, beggars needing to be fed.
Pray that our gates bring strangers.

Give away grain overflowing the silos,
press beggars in from the road and clothe them,
send riders to warn our cousins
beware of angels seeking work.

I Still Can't Say the Word

Simply sit still, if you must, and breathe.
Breathe in and let it out. Again. See how
the seconds crawl. Mumble the word you feel.
Or scream, yes, scream, beat wood, strip the flowers,

break the table if you must. But not your fist.
All right, your fist, then; if it breaks, it breaks.
That's good. No one can hold her breath like this
or beat a table like a metronome. Today

is almost dark, tomorrow will be gone.
We'll look back Saturday and call each week
tomorrow. Curse cars and alcohol
again, damn all drunk drivers, scream and shriek.

I'll never blame, no matter what you do.
Guns can't bring him back. I'd take this gun
and pistol-whip his face to jam, for you,
I'd break his bones and suck the marrow and blood

like siphoning raw gas, and spit the platelets
out, if that would save you. I'd skin him
like a deer and stitch it like a shield, if that
would bring back our boy, leap arm-locked with him

into the fire myself, if our son could live.
I've said it again and I mean it, but it's bald
as a lie. The facts are we are home, like this
together, grieving, and our son is gone.

When Baseball Was a Game

I lift my ball cap by the bill to scratch
and fingernail bald scalp. I never felt so old,
stiff knuckles cocked like runners on every base.

I haven't needed a cap since my last
good season with old men in the senior league.
I keep my Nelly Fox glove oiled and propped

in the closet, the pocket almost black,
an unscuffed baseball snug to hold the shape.
What luck, to play past sixty

while balding teammates took turns in surgery—
cancer, hernias, kidney stones.
I lift it again and squeeze the bill,

sweat stains indelible after sun
and a dozen washings, the F4 Phantom faded,
not the olive-green machine I flew decades ago.

Before Vietnam and the death of friends,
I could chase down a ball off the wall
and turn and hurl a strike three hundred feet

to a teammate blocking home plate,
the capless runner diving but hopelessly out,
the home crowd rising, going wild.

Fire and Ice

If it's August scorching,
buy blocks of ice,
the old kind, 25, 50 pounds.
Prop the pump house door
wide open. If it floods,
let it freeze. If it's ice,

take a torch. Upright
or on your knees, faith isn't easy,
all that sweet and fat,
a world of Cornish cream
and butcher shops.
Arteries clog like pipes

of mineral-hard West Texas water.
Faith's a laser-thin cable
for light, easy to kink,
like a cheap plastic garden hose.
A watt could heat your house,
melt the fatty glacier

clogging your heart.
Pin-prick a hole in cardboard,
turn your back on a solar eclipse.
Watch the shadow world
nibble your only sun,
but remember Lot's wife:

watch only the cardboard.
Scoffers will turn
and stare directly at the fire,
learning too late
their retinas are burned.
Lit by a birthday candle

at a thousand miles,
faith pings and jingles
like wind chimes on the patio,
like a telephone call
we've almost stopped expecting,
the gong of an entry bell.

Before the Glaciers Melt

Montana dawn holds up the moon,
off white and umber, the last
half nugget found above ground
in the Rockies. I pitch the tent flap back
and it crackles: I'm twenty again,

watching my bride in the bedroll.
Montana geese honk past us,
gliding to the lake. Honeymoon,
the dew so cold the fall grass snaps
when I step out, wildly in love with a girl

I believed would be that young forever.
But now we're back in Montana, at 65,
and here come the geese. Next year
it'll be 2000, glaciers melting fast
this side of the ice age. Another

hundred years, they'll all be gone.
Tourists in that millennium may come
in sleek, electric cars and wonder
why it was called Glacier Park,
like fossils in the park's museum.

They'll see eagles mounted in glass,
stuffed grizzlies rearing up
from the '90s, beasts they've read about
like dinosaurs. They'll pass a tent
like ours, and camp stools, a propane stove

and bedrolls, the quaint way
others camped long ago, like us.
Crouched, I pump the Coleman stove
and put the coffee on, strike a match
and watch the flames turn blue.

And now, inside the tent, my wife
unzips her sleeping bag, sits up
and brushes her gray lovely hair,
and I duck inside and kneel
with both mugs steaming in my fists.

Raising a Glass for Grandsons

Break out champagne Uncle Frank smuggled back
from France in 1918, dying childless.
He followed his heart and the zodiac,
believed he saw our daughter's star and blessed
her in his will, godfather of all
her children. Never mind the codicil:
she may have other sons, but these births call
for toasts: twins come once a lifetime, not skill

but grace, like rising after being hit
by lightning, or seeing Halley's comet twice.
Even Uncle Frank can't cancel the will
after the wine's been tasted. Tonight
we'll toast these ruddy babies and angels
dancing on threads above their cradles,
mobiles circling to ward off beasties
and ghosts, to shower both with health, to keep
their parents safe, to be here night
and day when these boys wake and cry.

Faith Is a Radical Master

Can that hummingbird
that slammed against the glass
believe invisible facts?

Does she wobble off
embarrassed and wary,
or dazed? After thousands of miles

on the Mexico flyway, through gusts
and over clouds, through rain,
she hit the glass storm door

like flying blind.
If her beak's not bent,
can she ever let it lead her

full speed to nectar,
the yellow gold of blooms?
Is God in the clear, after all,

not beyond, not hidden in clouds
I've stared at, but here
in my heart where I rise

like a blind man leaping
and shouting *Look!*
look, I can see!

Old Pilots in the Crowd
at Kitty Hawk

The guide says the mannequin with the mustache,
that's Orville. The guide's eyes twinkle
and he points. Orville's hanging head-first
into history, his left fist stiff on the controls.

Inside the visitors' center, the mock-up
never flies, just what scoffers always warned
those quacks from Ohio. Fake props are plastic,
the faces painted gaudy as corpses,

hard to feel for dummies in crash tests.
In grainy pictures, the brothers never smile,
but both look vulnerable and real. Wilbur,
we know, died young. The guide asks pilots

to raise our hands, and all who do
are old. We've all flown fighters, transports,
bombers that could wipe Kitty Hawk off the map,
turn the sandy Outer Banks to glass.

The guide's dramatic, grabs the wing
and twists, proving the skills of lift
and turn. We'd rather he step aside, let us roll
that old crate outside, flip for the right

to go first on our bellies. Goggles down,
cracked leather gloves tugged on, we'd nod,
face to the wind and history be damned,
full throttle at thirty miles an hour,

a hundred, eight hundred feet down range.
What was Wilbur's record that day, almost a minute?
Never mind the hedge of trees they've planted
a hundred feet beyond, watch this.

Five Fathoms Down off Hatteras

Can we believe this rubble, these rusted bolts?
Immigrants trusted iron, turned their backs
on Cornish cream and breezes, clambered up gangplanks
for bunks below deck aboard a wreck.

Did they guess disaster in the captain's eyes?
Did fields of barley and tobacco seem like gold,
worth risking shoals along the Outer Banks?
What did they hope the crew could do?

Did they imagine drowning near a beach
like this? Grandmother docked in Norfolk
the winter this British ship beached, broke up
in pounding surf. Boats went out from Hatteras

but found only boxes, not even a corpse.
Now, in scuba gear, we flip our feet like dolphins
that waver about like escorts, no sharks today,
no sharks. The planks are gone, the portholes

Cornish eyes looked through before sea water
forced them shut. They're down here
in the silt. Zebra fish swim wide-eyed
through the hull like uniformed guards,

Don't touch. Already the bottom shifts, drifts up
and covers rusted bolts we touched. In weeks
the wreck will all be lost again, discovered
years from now, or never. If we hover long enough,

rubbing each bolt and bulkhead, if we try to imagine
the last battered hours, each desperate wife's
and child's, the surf will still take it back,
hide this massive iron again in silt.

Boiling Shells at Kitty Hawk

Back home, my wife will lace them into wreaths,
glue-gun the shells as bouquets for neighbors—
Scotch Bonnets, conches, glossy moonsnails curled
like custard cones. Boiling, they smell like lobster,

the condo opened to a gale that cracks the breakers back.
No dolphins leap and pirouette today, no swans.
Gulls flap and sidle, laws of yaw and roll as old as wings.
Orville rode two pusher props twelve seconds over dunes

a mile from here, nine decades ago today. At noon,
I measured the path of his flight, takeoff to touchdown,
no farther than hop-skip-and-jump when I was a boy.
Four decades ago, I soloed, when Saigon and Da Nang

were distant, exotic towns. The Wrights launched me
to madness. Hurtling down that track at twenty knots,
did Orville worry about war, the rubble bombs would cause?
Or was he giddy like me that first roll down a runway,

ready for anything, anything? Firewall the pistons, nose up
and let it lift. All roads led to Rome, but runways
started here near the beach of my father's boyhood.
All my father's friends from World War I are dead,

the Wrights are dead, and many friends I flew with
in Vietnam. I've touched their names in granite on a wall.
Now, I don't fly, except at night in orbits that won't stop.
Turn out the fire and let the boiled pot cool.

Lay out the mussels, slippershells, the angel wings
and let them dry, then pack them like bone china
in paper towels. Even periwinkles last if padded,
enough for a wreath for some good neighbor's wall.

Watching Dawn on Padre Island

From the deck, sunrise splashes the Gulf,
glistens like a highway paved with gold.
The condo's garden sprawls like seaweed
flattened by the breeze. Salt sprays the balcony,
chairs sticky with brine. Lazy as Lazarus,

I lounge with my wife, weeks after doctors
sawed my chest bones wide and lifted out my heart.
Holding hands, we watch the waves, the sandhill cranes,
beaks to the wind like weather vanes. Last month,
I listened to neighbors telling fables of near-death,

as if words would console me—a light so bright,
agony wouldn't matter. Maybe like this blazing stairway
to the sun, glittering over millions of sharks
and tarpons. The glare's so bright I'm blind,
and flip sunglasses down from my scalp and blink.

Pain makes surgery easy—a silly, giddy relief,
a straw to grab for, touch of a master's hand—
easy, wheeled down the hall to a bright-lit room
that dazzles, forbidden to friends, to family.
I remember counting back, then odd confusion

in a recovery room, like waking dazed in a cave
or casket, bright light and voices, but whose?
And what were they saying, what happened
and where was this, wondering why can't I rise
and throw off these winding sheets and walk.